. . . you've become
a bit more
extroverted.

YOU KNOW YOU'RE GROWN UP WHEN...

By Jeanne Hanson

Illustrated by
Lee Lorenz

Workman Publishing
New York

To my parents.
J.H.

Library of Congress Cataloging-in-Publication Data
Hanson, Jeanne K.
You Know You're Grown Up When . . . / Jeanne K.
Hanson; illustrated by Lee Lorenz.

1. Men—Psychology—Humor. 2. Middle aged men—
Psychology—Humor. 3. American wit and humor. I. Lorenz,
Lee. II. Title.

PN6231.M45H3   1991   818'.5402—dc20   91-50383
CIP

Published by
Workman Publishing
708 Broadway
New York, NY 10003

10 9 8 7 6 5 4 3 2 1

ISBN 1-56305-115-X

Time to Celebrate!

Being grown up is nothing to whine about or wax apologetic about. And it's certainly nothing to defer to young people about. Just the opposite! Wiser than the elephant, craftier than the crow, more powerful than the wolf, we grown-ups know who we are and what's important in life. We know the shape of the world and understand the people in it. We know our own goals and limitations. And we know all the best ways to have fun.

You'll know you're grown up, too, if you recognize yourself in the pages that follow—and find yourself secretly smiling at your own self-portrait.

Your mother no longer sets out toothpaste for you when you visit.

Your father shows an interest in your career.

You've taken your parents out to dinner.

You realize you'll always
be afraid of bats . . .

or snakes . . .

or moths (big ones) . . .

or all of the above.

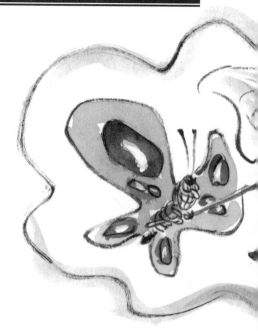

YOU KNOW YOU'RE GROWN UP WHEN ...

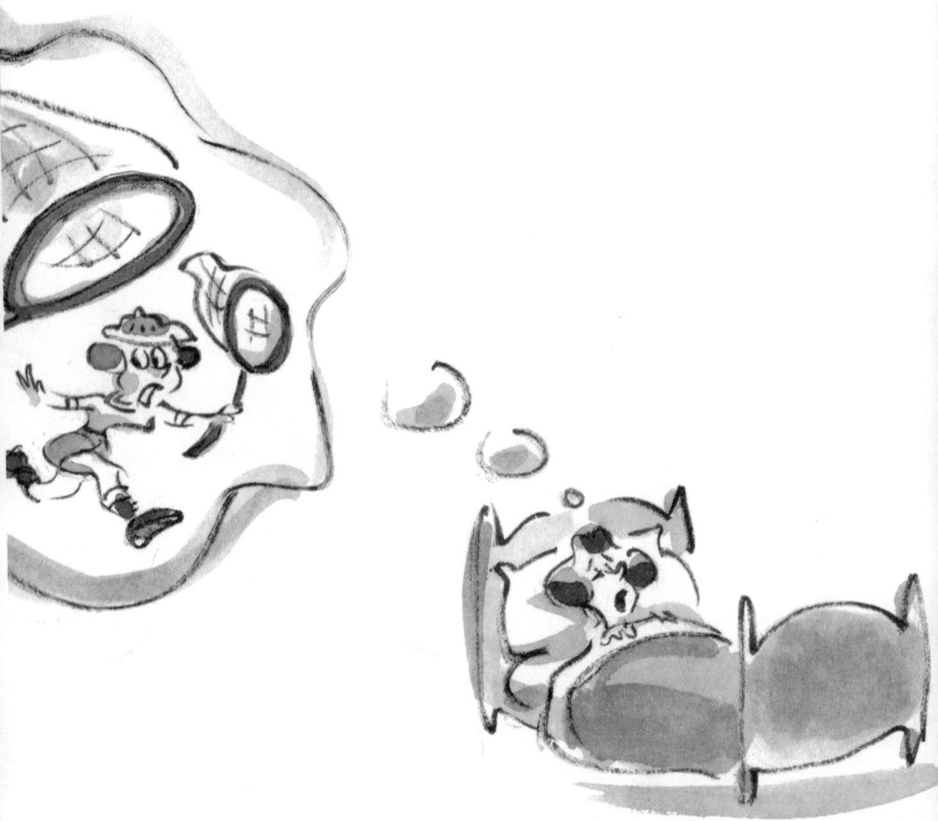

A lot of people at work are coming to you for career advice.

You understand better than ever the importance of office politics.

You really, really
love your pet.
And, yes, your cat is
starting to look like you
(but not vice versa).

You wonder if you might be too old to wear your Saturday painter overalls in public . . .

  or take up wind-surfing . . .

  or cruise a singles bar.

You're sick to death of some of the dummies at work.

You recognize the importance of laughter.

You decide that you've always wanted to have sex on the beach—and you finally do it.

You notice that people you meet at parties seem to admire your mind as much as your body.

Your mother or father, or both, look like saints for what they put up with from you.

You realize that your parents were right about a lot of things.

You're less embarrassed by weird relatives.

You look forward to family reunions.

You're believing more in the influence of heredity.

You enjoy being
a matchmaker.

You know you hate rap music.

You're bored with board games.

You think some of the people you hang around with are kind of superficial.

You're thinking about having an affair, or getting married, whichever isn't already in progress.

You see people your age becoming cynical and you don't want that to happen to you.

You begin to value moderation over a life of wild excess.

You're more opinionated (but better at hiding it).

You and your spouse are starting to use a few gimmicks in the bedroom.

You can spot a phony a mile away.

You're confident in your intuitions and gut feelings.

YOU KNOW YOU'RE GROWN UP WHEN ...

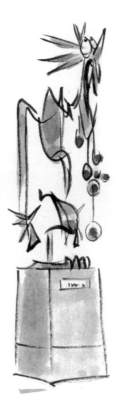

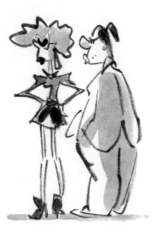

You realize that love
does mean having to
say you're sorry.

You're getting really sick of people with inflated egos, especially at work.

You don't like most of the new hairstyles.

You've started thinking about going into business for yourself.

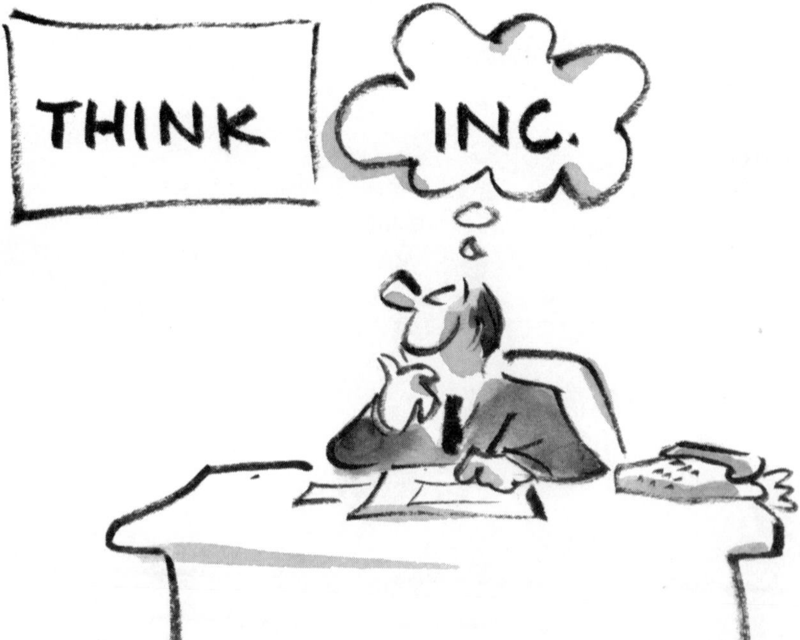
THINK
INC.

The snoring of your significant other sounds like a buzz saw.

You think some people your age wear too much makeup.

Your family is more important to you than your friends.

You're thinking about smiling more because wrinkles don't look as bad as frown lines!

You're tired of moving . . .

    and trendy food . . .

    and other people's children.

You don't care as much about what people think of you.

You know how to pick your battles at work.

You've become a bit sentimental.

You're an interesting blend of restless and settled.

You no longer believe that people can change themselves radically.

You're getting "more so."

You wish your grandparents were still around to talk to.

You don't like junk food as much as you used to.

You've become
a bit more
extroverted.

Candlelight does more for your looks than ever before.

You like a quiet evening at home.

You find it less difficult to forgive people.

Your "little cousin" has become a successful lawyer.

Your "baby brother" is getting a divorce.

You're getting hand-me-downs from your children.

You've accepted that your parents are getting old.

You appreciate holidays more:
    Thanksgiving, Valentine's Day, and birthdays
    (especially a friend's).

You're really sick of New Year's Eve.

You find it harder to lose weight.

You're more annoyed at interruptions.

Your spouse or significant other has a few gray hairs and you think it actually looks distinguished.

You've given up on changing your spouse's bad habits (well, pretty much).

You think a divorce sounds way too expensive.

You understand the expression "Life's too short for . . . "

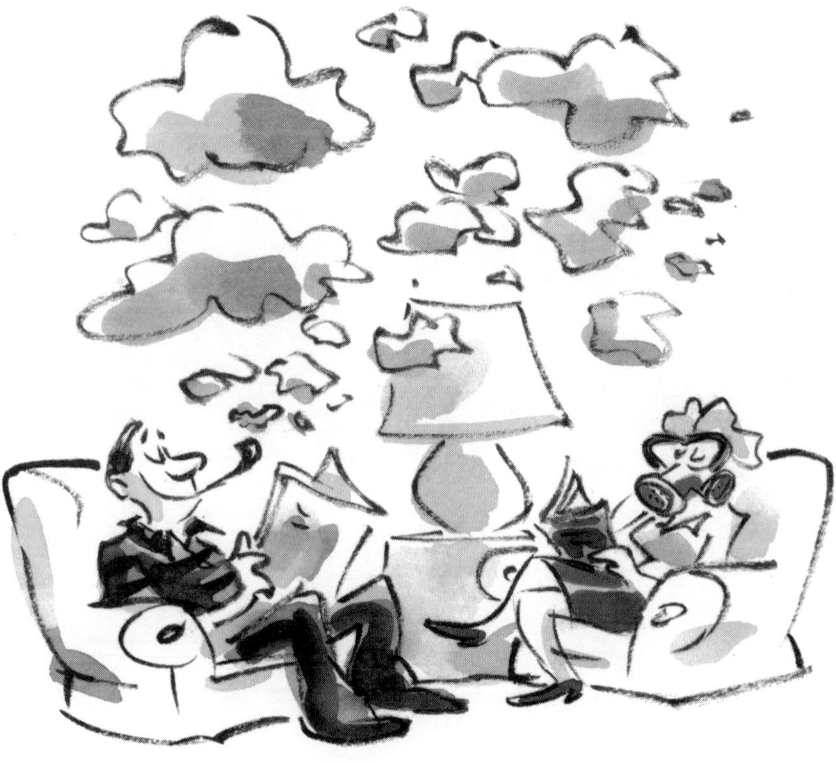

You begin to think of your possessions as heirlooms for your children.

You know you should be saving more money.

What used to be tempting has become *more* tempting.

You find yourself attracted to people who have your same body type.

You'd like to take a year off from your job (but be able to return to it if you want to).

You can swallow those four little words: "I told you so."

You're better at keeping secrets.

Young men with really bulky muscles look dumb to you.

You have more sympathy for other people's troubles.

You know you aren't perfect
and it doesn't bother you.

You realize that you have

　　your father's smile,

　　your uncle's work habits,

　　and your grandmother's temper.

You find yourself holding forth to your children on the virtues of capitalism.

You know you'll never run a marathon . . .
    or own a villa in the South of France . . .
    or control General Motors . . .
and it doesn't bother you.

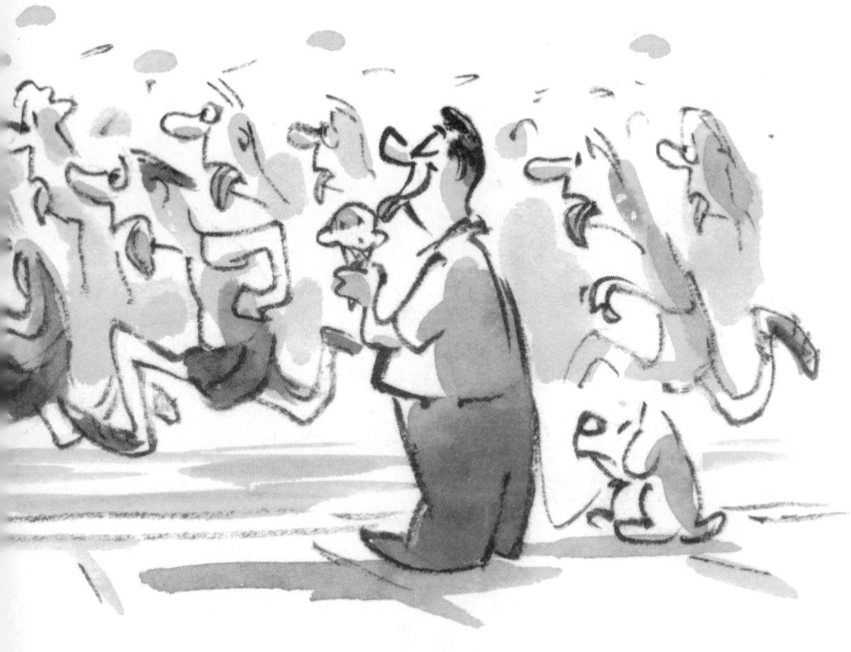

You sometimes surprise yourself by thinking about owning another house or having another child.

You no longer lust after a red sports car or a spouse who is 20 years younger.

You want sex to be sweet rather than athletic.

Those ads for patent medicines don't seem so stupid anymore.

You like small dinner parties better than large mill-arounds.

You think some of your clothes are getting boring.

You'd like to start collecting something.

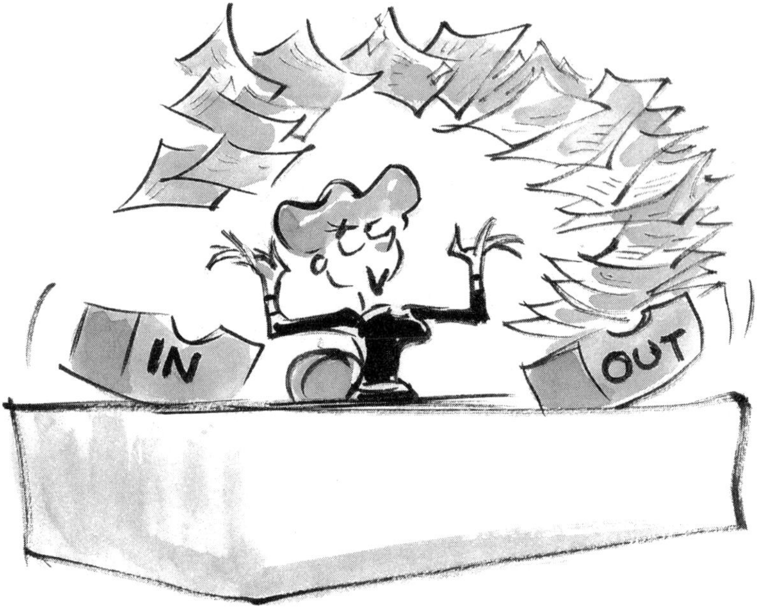
IN
OUT

You are, in fact, dazzlingly competent at your work.

The summer seems even shorter,
   and the fall,
   and the winter,
   and the spring . . .
Where did last
   year go?

You don't like shopping anymore.

You're better at setting priorities.

You think about comfort as well as looks when you're buying new shoes.

You don't want to suffer fools gladly, but you realize that sometimes you must.

You know certain colors and patterns will *never* look good on you.

It's appealing to ponder
becoming eccentric someday.

YOU KNOW YOU'RE GROWN UP WHEN ...

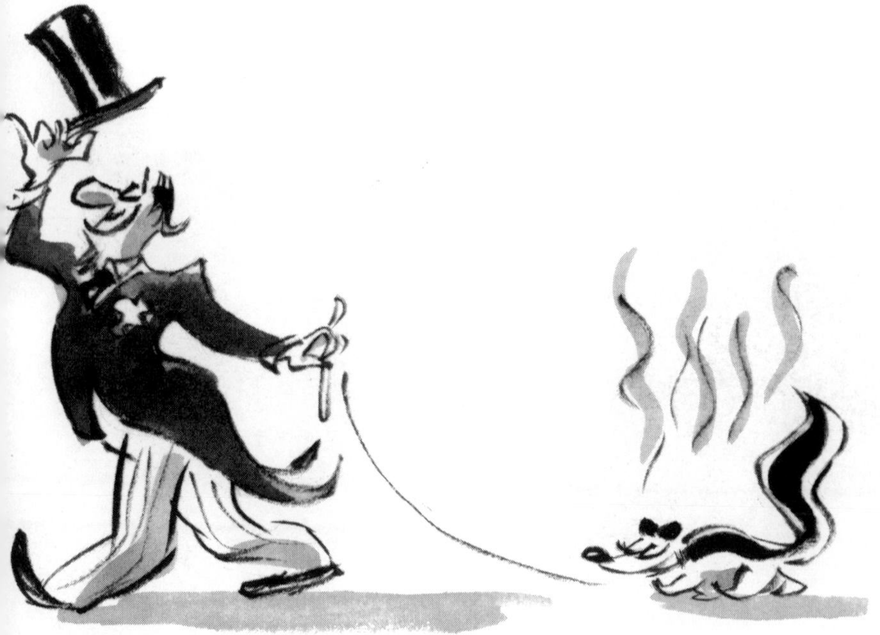

You find that getting angry is usually a waste of time.

You're developing some pet peeves.

You have almost *too* many contacts.

You find yourself sleeping less.

You value qualities in people besides looks and "good personality"—such as

energy,

steadfastness,

a sense of humor.

Bird-watching doesn't
sound like such a
corny hobby after all.

Your muscles hurt after . . .
   vacuuming the stairs,
   and grooming the dog,
   and washing the car.

You're spending more time on financial planning.

Your children can program the VCR,

   and fix the answering machine,

   and play Nintendo games,

and you can't.

You're far more finicky about germs.

Your golf or tennis game (or whatever) is getting quite impressive.

Some foods no longer agree with you all the time . . .

roast beef sandwiches,

vinegary salad dressing,

even pepperoni pizza.

You think you'd like to learn (or relearn) a foreign language.

You start to think walking is exercise.

You need more coffee to wake up in the morning, especially in wintertime.

You've given up trying to
get the perfect tan.

You realize you'll never be thin,

or tall,

or effortlessly athletic,

and you've accepted it (pretty much).

You understand how sexual-role expectations have shaped your life.

You find certain things about the opposite sex more irritating than ever (but others are still quite charming).

You realize that it's some of the nerdy types from everybody's high school class who are now running the country.

COMPUTER WHIZ
SCIENTIST
HUMANITARIAN
PHILANTHROPIST
BUT STILL A
NERD

You're exercising and watching your diet for more than just your appearance.

You know there are no more alibis—for yourself or other people.

Older people don't seem that old anymore.

You're less wasteful.

You love to travel — more than ever before.

You decide to make more time for your hobby.

You like history better than you used to.

You're (even) less superficial.

And you know (better than ever) how to love.